C000174821

THE QUANTOCKS

Brian Pearce

First published in Great Britain in 2009
Reprinted in 2016

British Library Cataloguing-in-Publication Data
A CIP record for this title is available from the British Library

ISBN 978 1 906887 14 8

PiXZ Books
Halsgrove House, Ryelands Business Park,
Bagley Road, Wellington, Somerset TA21 9PZ
Tel: 01823 653777
Fax: 01823 216796
email: sales@halsgrove.com

An imprint of Halstar Ltd, part of the Halsgrove group of companies
Information on all Halsgrove titles is available at: www.halsgrove.com

Printed in China by Toppan Leefung Printing Ltd

Contents

How to use this book

The Area

The Quantocks was one of the first areas to be designated an Area of Outstanding Natural Beauty. There were earlier plans to include it in Exmoor National Park. It shares with the latter the Devonian red sandstones and the indigenous red deer and ponies. The Quantocks afford drier walking than the boggy Exmoor plateau, although much depends upon weather conditions.

The eastern edge of the Quantocks is heavily forested but the main area of forestry, along with most of the open heathland, is open access. The most recent Ordnance Survey Explorer maps show such areas. This means that you are free to wander over a large proportion of the hills. They provide stunning views northwards over the Bristol Channel to Wales, eastwards over Bridgwater to the Somerset Levels and Mendips, southwards over Taunton to the Blackdowns and westwards over the Vale of Taunton Deane to the Brendon Hills and Exmoor. So, try to pick clear days for your walks.

Although it is essentially a heathland area, perhaps the most memorable aspect of the Quantocks is its trees. Be it the gnarled and twisted oaks on Dowsborough, the towering firs of Ramscombe, the beech hedgebanks, the tree-lined prehistoric ridgeway track or the charm of the gently wooded Holford Combe, you cannot fail to be impressed by the trees. It will become obvious why the area attracted poets such as Coleridge, Wordsworth and Newbolt and how they delighted in woodland walks.

The Routes

All the routes are circular and of moderate length. They vary from four to seven and a half miles and are graded from one to three boots – from easy to more challenging. The routes are intended to pass places for refreshment, and all but the Aisholt walk do this. However, the Quantocks is a ridge and most refreshment places are in villages below the ridge. Thus all walks involve uphill and downhill sections. The walks from East Quantoxhead and Stogursey, however, are designed to take the walker away from the ridge to provide some gentler gradients. None are suitable for buggies or wheelchairs.

The Quantocks is a popular recreational area for residents of surrounding towns. It is criss-crossed by bridleways used by riders and mountain bikers. Many tracks are also byways, which may be open to all traffic or on which vehicles are restricted. There is a tradition of use by off road vehicles on the top of the ridge. Although the main ridge provides classic walking and superb views, enjoyment can be spoilt by the intensity of use by other users, so our routes do not dwell on this area.

The routes make much use of the Quantock Greenway. This is a clearly way-marked route circling the Quantocks with a link across the ridge in the middle so that it forms two loops. It is designed to take pressure off the main ridge routes but still provides good walking. Some routes also follow the Coleridge Way, with its distinctive quill waymark. This starts at Coleridge's house at Nether Stowey and goes to Holford, where his friend Wordsworth lived, and to West Quantoxhead and Bicknoller before going on to Exmoor. It is not designed as a challenge but as a leisurely walk from which the participants can take inspiration from the landscape as the poets did.

The main ridge is followed by two other long distance routes: the Macmillan Way West and the Samaritans Way South West. These are designed as challenge routes for sponsored walks to raise money for the respective charities. The West Somerset Coast Path, with its ammonite fossil waymark, is a link between the South West Coast Path at Minehead and the River Parrett Trail at Steart. It comes inland to West Quantoxhead.

Our routes all follow these designated trails or public rights of way. Such routes are subject to change or diversion. Some routes inevitably include sections of tarmaced roads. Busy roads have been avoided, except to cross them at a couple of points. It is the roads that are the most dangerous parts of the routes. Follow the convention and keep in to the right hand side of roads in single file. As all routes touch roads, they are mostly accessible by public transport. Timetable details are available on www.travelinesw.com or www.firstgroup.com

The Maps

Our sketch maps and route description can only be a rough guide to each walk. The Quantocks are criss-crossed by a network of trails, paths and sheep tracks. A detailed map and the skill to use it are essential, especially if you stray from the route or are forced to make a short cut. Only one map is necessary: the Ordnance Survey Explorer Map 140 (Quantock Hills and Bridgwater). These are available in a waterproof format if required. For availability, access www.ordnancesurvey.co.uk/leisure

You will need to be able to use a grid reference to find the start of each walk. A postcode is also given to aid some satellite navigation systems and this is particularly useful to inform emergency services if necessary. Compass directions are given in brackets for some route sections. A compass would, therefore, be a useful aid to navigation.

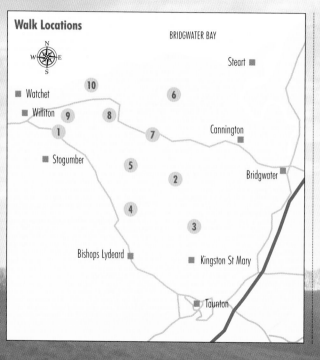

Walk Locations

BRIDGWATER BAY

Steart ■

① ② ③ ④ ⑤ ⑥ ⑦ ⑧ ⑨ ⑩

■ Watchet
■ Williton

Cannington ■

■ Stogumber

Bridgwater ■

Bishops Lydeard ■

■ Kingston St Mary

■ Taunton

Key to Symbols Used

Level of difficulty:
Easy 🐾
Moderate 🐾 🐾

Map symbols:
🚗 Park & start
⬚⬚⬚ Tarred Road
– – – Footpath
▬ ▬ ▬ Walk Footpath
■ Building
+ Church
▲ Triangulation pillar or other landmark
🚻 WC
🍽 Refreshments
🍺 Pub

1 Bicknoller

A walk including classic Quantock scenery of wooded combes and open heaths, with views on both sides of the ridge.

Level: 🐾 🐾
Length: 10 kms, 6.5 miles
Terrain: Over the ridge and back provides two climbs with one stiff section.
Park and start: Village hall car park behind hall and shop. It says private but can be used by public for honesty box contribution.
Start ref: ST 111396. Postcode TA4 4EL
Public transport: Good but to turn for Bicknoller on A358
Websites: www.bicknoller.com
www.quantockonline.co.uk/quantocks/villages
www.quantockhills.com

Worth a short detour, the church is the main feature of note in Bicknoller. The churchyard has stocks under an ancient yew tree, a pound for stray animals and an unusually complete 14th century cross. A row of seven tombstones commemorates the Bickham family, famed for their huge parties, after which they sometimes shot at the weathercock on the church tower. The holes in it can still be seen.

Local farmers relied heavily on the common grazing and were allowed to graze as many sheep on the heath in summer as they could feed on their own turnips in winter. The heath has always changed with fortunes in agriculture. Much shows the 'ridge and furrow' marks of medieval ploughing. It was ploughed to take crops for a couple of seasons before letting it revert, although it was never the same again.

7

Bicknoller Church

1 **Set off:** Turn left out of the car park and go up Hill Lane opposite. Go through the gate at the end of the road and turn right along the Greenway. Continue along the edge of open country for half a mile.

2 At some houses, turn right and go down the road for two hundred yards. At the road junction turn left along the lane following the Greenway signs. Look back to Trendle

Bicknoller Inn

Ring on the hillside. Continue for half a mile, past Thorncombe House, and turn left at the bridleway sign.

3 Take the track up Paradise Combe. After a quarter of a mile, after a left hand bend, take the unsigned path across the stream to the right. Keep upwards through the bracken and round into the next

Known as a 'hill slope enclosure' Trendle Ring is one of the best known examples of this type of structure. It is presumed to be an Iron Age settlement but nothing is known of its function. 'Trendle' is an Old English name for a circle or hoop.

Thorncombe Hill

Hallsway Hill looking towards Black Hill

Halsway Post

combe aiming (E) at the top corner of the beech hedgebank ahead.

4 Follow the hedge around for two hundred yards, then bearing up to the left (NE), heading around the tops of combes to the low point of the main ridge. There you will come to Halsway Post.

5 Cross the ridge with the post to your right and drop (NE) into the combe ahead, taking the track along the left hand valley side. Half a mile from the post the track hooks around a side combe and drops right handed (N) to the bottom of the wooded Somerton Combe. Half a mile onwards, bear left where another combe joins.

Halsway Post is one of a series of timber posts doubling as parish boundary and location markers at track junctions on open heathland. The current Halsway and Bicknoller Posts are made from local oak and were installed on the site of previous posts in 2008.

Beech trees above Paradise Combe

6 Cross the stream and head up (W) this combe (Sheppard's Combe) for a mile. The path winds up to the main ridge at Bicknoller Post.

7 At the post bear sharp left (SW). Cross the main track running along the ridge and head for the top of a small rise, a hundred yards ahead. Continue over the top, cross another path and drop to the head of deep Bicknoller Combe. Turn right and drop down the bottom of the combe for a mile. This brings you back to the gate at Hill Lane. Go through and return down the lane to the car park.

Top
Bicknoller Combe
Right
Sheppard's Combe

From Bicknoller Post Hinkley Point power station commands the view to the NE. Beyond can be seen the mouth of the Parrett, Brent Knoll and the Mendips and, moving to the left, Weston–Super-Mare, the islands of Steepholm and Flatholm, the Welsh coast, Williton, Minehead and Exmoor.

2 **Aisholt**

A contrasting walk of variety with a gentle walk around a beautiful reservoir, a tiny Quantock village and a climb into the forested and heat-covered hillsides.

The poet Sir Henry Newbolt called Aisholt "that beloved valley". He wished the village would remain unspoiled, and, tucked away without a shop, pub or parking area, it is. Coleridge described the valley as a 'green romantic chasm' and would have lived there but for the lack of amenities his wife Sara wanted. As he wrote to his benefactor, Thomas Poole of Nether Stowey: "The situation is delicious; all I could wish, but Sara being Sara, and I being I, we must live in a town or else close to one, so that she may have neighbours and acquaintances. For my friends form not that society which is of itself sufficient to a woman."

Level: 🐾 🐾
Length: 11 kms, 6.5 miles but route forms two loops, so can be shortened
Terrain: A walk of two halves: easy going around reservoir and more strenuous around Aisholt Common, with paths that are wet and muddy in winter.
Park and start: Lay-by beside Hawkridge Reservoir, a mile and a half south west of Spaxton village.
Start ref: ST207361. Postcode TA5 1AL
Public transport: None
Websites:
www.quantockonline.co.uk/quantocks/villages
www.wessexwater.co.uk

Aisholt Common

1 **Set off:** Facing the reservoir, turn right and follow the road. After the cottage, turn left, taking the footpath into the field. Drop to a track. Follow this past the landing stage and clubhouse into an open area with seats.

2 Drop down left to the track to the dam. Do not go to the dam but at the hedge bear right over a stile into a field. Drop right handed (NE) down to the stream. Go through the woods and at the road turn left to drop down to the cottage.

3 At the cottage the path goes up to the left of the garages and round behind them. The path bears right, then left following the edge of the plantation. It then enters a field and follows the hedge to the left, taking a stile to the left into the next field then up and along the edge of the woodland to a crossing of paths.

4 Do not go through the gates but drop gradually down to

Newbolts Cottage

Aisholt Wood

Hawkridge Reservoir, finished in 1962, supplies water for Bridgwater. At the western end is a settling pond that is home to large numbers of toads. Between February and April many cross the causeway into the main part of the reservoir.

Aisholt Church

The ancient oak woodland of Aisholt Wood is managed by Somerset Wildlife Trust and it has open access. The wood was heavily coppiced for charcoal and the oaks for tannin. 'Broomsquires', made besoms. The handles were made of ash or oak, the bristles of birch and the bindings of willow or bramble.

the reservoir (SW) keeping the field boundary to your right. The route eventually becomes a track dropping to a road. Here the route can be cut short by bearing left along the pavement and following it round the reservoir back to the car park.

(5) Cross the road by the causeway over the reservoir and take the bridleway opposite. Follow the valley upwards, within half a mile fording the stream into Aisholt Wood.

(6) Keep up the main track and out onto a road by a thatched cottage. Turn left up the road to Aisholt church.

(7) Take the gate by Shepherd's Cottage opposite the church steps. In the field turn left and go up the steps into the next field. Bear right and follow the field boundary for 600 yards. Ford the stream to come out onto a road in front of Holcombe Cottage.

(8) Turn left up the road. At Durborough Farm turn right,

through a gate, and follow the bridleway by the stream (can be very wet). In 250 yards the track opens into woodland. You are now on Aisholt Common, which is open access. The walk can be shortened by roughly following the edge of open country up to the right but the route is indistinct in the woodland. Otherwise, continue up the track for half a mile. At the edge

In the 1930s the thatched cottage, known as The Old Scholhouse, was lived in by the poet and novelist Sir Henry Newbolt. 'Drake's Drum' is probably his most famous poem but he wrote many influential works about servicemen in the First World War.

Aisholt Common

Track near Princites Covert

of the woodland bear right (NW), up a steep combe for another half mile. At the top you come to a broad track running along the edge of a plantation.

 9 Turn right and follow the track downhill for two miles.

Bridleway Durborough

At the road keep ahead for another half mile. Just before a road junction turn back down to the right along a bridleway. This drops to meet a track through the woods that you have already walked. Turn left to return to the road by the causeway over the reservoir. Cross the road, and turn right, following the pavement round to the left at the road junction and back to the car park.

The lonely site, together with the shape and size of the nave suggests that the first church at Aisholt was a Dark Age hermitage. Life in early 19th century Aisholt is brought to life through the diaries of a former vicar, William Holland, published under the title of Paupers and Pig Killers.

3 Broomfield

A walk around the gentler slopes of the SE end of the Quantock ridge but rising to Cothelstone Hill with stunning views on a fine day.

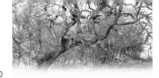

Collinson, the Somerset historian, writing at the end of the eighteenth century, said of Broomfield: "It is beautifully varied, with swelling hills and deep romantic vales, and commanding a great variety of pleasing landscapes and very extensive prospects. Broomfield is a shrunken settlement, with many former dwellings in ruins due to the slump in agriculture in the late 19th and early 20th centuries. A village hall remains but the school and post office are long gone. In the porch of the church are interesting details of local charities. One states that: "honest workmen" may apply for free tools if they have not pawned those given to them in the previous year! The green outside was once site of a famed fair for the sale of Dorset Horn sheep.

Level: 🐾 🐾
Length: 11 kms, 7 miles
Terrain: One long, gradual climb and one short, stiff one; can be muddy at times.
Park and start: Car park at Fyne Court. Be aware of closing times. Park near Broomfield village green if you may be late back.
Start ref: ST222322. Postcode TA5 2EQ
Public transport: None
Websites: www.quantockhills.com
www.quantockonline/quantocks/villages
www.nationaltrust.org/main/wfynecourt

Born in Fyne Court in 1784, Andrew Crosse died in the same bed in 1855. An amateur scientist with an interest in electricity, he was known locally as 'Wizard Crosse' or 'The Thunder and Lightning Man'. He was falsely accused of Frankenstein type experiments for the creation of life.

Map labels: End, Traveller's Rest, Broomfield Hill, Merridge Hill, The Pines, Cothelstone Hill, Ivyton Farm, Raswell Farm, Fyne Court

19

Folly at Fyne Court

In 1894 Fyne Court burnt
down, leaving the
outbuildings used now, in
National Trust ownership, as
a visitor centre and ranger
office. The grounds, now
crossed by nature trails,
were landscaped by the
Crosse family in the 18th
century and include an
arboretum, a complex leat
system and several ponds,
one with a boathouse folly
and a castle folly, used by
the Crosse children as a
play house.

Set off: From the car park return to the road. Here you may detour left to visit the church. Otherwise, turn right, then right at the next junction.

After a hundred yards, turn left down a track signed as the Greenway and Macmillan Way. After a quarter of a mile, fork right, following these signs down and up to the road beyond Raswell Farm.

Fyne Court Visitor Centre

Sunken Lane to Raswell Farm (right)

Cross the road and continue uphill on the Greenway.

(3) At the next road bear left along the road to Ivyton Farm. Pass the farmhouse on your right and keep along the lane. In half a mile you come to a junction in a rock cutting.

(4) Fork right and follow the lane uphill for a mile. Bear left where this rejoins the Macmillan Way along the edge of a plantation. Keep ahead, following the Macmillan Way signs through a gate onto heathland. Keep following these signs diagonally upwards to the left (NW) to the mound on the top of Cothelstone Hill.

(5) From the summit bear left (SW) down the ridge to an enclosed barrow. Follow the Macmillan Way signs down to the right and into woodland. Keep following the signs downhill (NE) to the crossroads at Park End. Cross the road to the right of the crossroads and follow the track through the woods. Keep ahead and downwards at the crossing of tracks, continuing to a road.

(6) Cross the road and go down the road opposite, past Manor Farm and up to the road junction. Turn left, past the Traveller's Rest and, at the junction beyond, turn right on a footpath on a lane running up the hill.

On the top of Cothelstone Hill is a ring of beech trees called the Seven Sisters. Collinson wrote: "the eye commands 14 counties and, with a glass on a clear day, 150 churches."

Cothelstone Hill from Broomfield Hill

Walkers on Cothelstone Hill

7 At the top of the hill continue past the National Trust sign and down into the woods, with the field boundary on your left. You pass some huge beech trees before reaching a road. Turn left and go down the road for a mile, following signs for Fyne Court to return to the car park.

From Broomfield Hill you can look to the west along the Quantock ridge from Cothelstone Hill to Beacon Hill. To the north you can look into Wales as far as the Brecon Beacons.

Above and below: Cothelstone Hill

Beacon Hill from Broomfield Hill

4 **West Bagborough**

A walk climbing to the highest point on the Quantocks, best for views on a clear day, taking in a village, two pubs and a mixture of scenery.

Level: 🐾 🐾
Length: 8 kms, 5 miles
Terrain: A mix of open heath, woodland and farmland with one stiff climb.
Park and start: No car park but park where road widens below Rising Sun inn
Start ref: ST170334. Postcode TA4 3EF
Public transport: Reasonable (to West Bagborough)
Websites: www.quantockhills.com
www.quantockonline.co.uk/quantocks/villages
www.west-bagborough.co.uk
www.blueballinn.co.uk

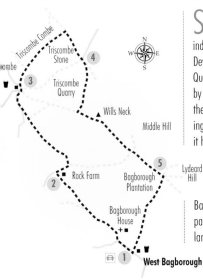

Simply known as 'Bagborough', the village once relied on the woollen industry for employment. The red Devonian gritstone from Triscombe Quarry was used mainly for road stone by the Tarmac company, notably for the runway at Heathrow. Work extracting stone stopped in 1999, since when it has been a nature reserve.

The landscape around the village has been greatly influenced by the inhabitants of Bagborough House. There is extensive parkland below the house and woodland above. West Bagborough Common was legally enclosed in 1810 and the result was for the owners of the house to buy up the allotments of the commoners and plant trees on the land.

Deer on Bagborough Hill

Set off: Go down the road below the pub. Where it bears left after the war memorial, follow the Greenway signs through the lych gate ahead, up into the churchyard and to the left. The path runs alongside a walled garden. Keep following the Greenway signs along fields for over half a mile. When you get to the track to Rock Farm, do not take the track but navigate carefully over the fields to join a lane below the farm.

The church of St Pancras stands to one side of the village, owing this separation to the Black Death, which reduced the population to below one hundred in the fourteenth century. The villagers abandoned the original settlement and re-built, away from the church.

Turn right and follow the lane up past the farm and through a gate into the woods. Bear left, following the Greenway signs along the edge of the woods for half a mile to a road. Continue ahead along the road,

Bagborough House, built in 1739, it has always been in the hands of the Popham family. It is a beautiful example of a Georgian country house and featured in the film Pandaemonium, a story of the relationship between Coleridge and Wordsworth.

Bagborough Church and House

which winds around the Blue Ball inn. Take the road to the right, running (N) ahead from the entrance to the pub.

Triscombe Stone is thought to date from the Bronze Age. The word 'Tris' is Celtic for 'meeting' and it is possible that the stone marks an ancient meeting place at the crossing of the 'Drove' Road and the old 'coaching' road from Watchet to Lyme Regis.

Triscombe Stone

In a hundred yards, where the road bears left, take the track running up past the house to the right. Keep upwards, through a gate and up the bottom of a steep combe. Keep onwards and upwards for half a mile until you reach the beech-lined track along the ridge on the top. Bear right along the track to the car park at Triscombe Stone.

 Keep ahead along the track and through a gate. After about a hundred yards of plantation

At 384m (1260 feet) above sea level, Wills Neck is the highest point of the Quantocks. The name may mean the neck of land belonging to the Wealas – the Welsh or ancient Britons. The summit provides views of Dartmoor, Exmoor, the Mendips, the Brecon Beacons, the Blackdown Hills, and into Dorset.

Dunkery Beacon from Wills Neck

on your left, bear right up a track running up the hill ahead. Near the top it joins another track. Bear left for the summit.

(5) At the summit keep ahead (SE) and down the track along the ridge. This brings you down to a plantation surrounded by a beech hedge. Take the track ahead (SE) along the edge of the plantation with the beech hedge to your right. Just before the gate and stile at the end of the hedge, drop down the track to the right. This brings you back down to the Rising Sun.

Formerly known as the 'Shepherd's Crook', the 'Rising Sun', a 16th century inn, was destroyed by fire in 2002 but has since been sympathetically rebuilt.

Stile on Lydeard Hill

5 **Quantock Forest**

A walk over the main ridge of the Quantocks and back, taking in forest drives with huge Douglas fir and hemlock trees and wide views to the west towards Exmoor.

Ramscombe is part of the 3000 acre Quantock Forest, managed since 1927 by the Forestry Commission. Somerset County Council purchased the Quantock Lodge Estate from a timber merchant who had felled the former oakwood for the war effort during the First World War. Great Wood once provided hardwood timber for shipbuilding and charcoal making. There are records of planting of pine and larch from the 18th century and the forest now produces softwood timber for paper making and building.

In 1949 the Friends of Quantock society was formed to combat further expansion of forestry. The turning point was the public reaction against the clear felling of ancient oaks in Hodder's Combe to make way for conifers. The expansion of plantation was checked and the landscaping and improvement of existing plantation for amenity began.

Level: 🥾 🥾
Length: 8 kms, 5 miles
Terrain: A mixture of plantation and open heath with one gradual climb and one shorter but steep climb.
Park and start: By toilets at Ramscombe car park. Ramscombe is signed from Adscombe, just south of Over Stowey, which is a mile south of Nether Stowey. Several parking and picnic areas in the forest.
Start ref: ST168377. Postcode TA5 1HN
Public transport: None
Websites: www.quantockonline.co.uk
www.quantockhills.com

Ramscombe

Crowcombe
Combe Gate

Fire
Beacon

Quantock
Farm

Quantock Combe

Adscombe

Great
Wood

Great Hill

tle
ntock
rm

Triscombe

Triscombe
Quarry

Ramscombe

Set off: With the toilets to your back, turn left and follow the track up the bottom of the combe. In 300 yards you pass the point where the road doubles back. Keep up the combe with the stream on your left for the next mile. The track comes out onto heathland and meets another track running alongside a road at the top. Turn left (SW) and follow the track to where it meets the road by a cattle grid (Crowcombe Park Gate).

Pony, Crowcombe Park Gate

Harepath, Crowcombe Park Gate

2 Cross the cattle grid and take the gate to the left. Follow the track, bearing right handed along the edge of the gorse to a ridge. Bear left (SE) at the low point of the ridge, cross the ridge and drop to a combe. Go through a gate onto a track and turn right. Follow the track down the combe for a quarter of a mile. Just before the farm bear left and upwards to follow the edge of open country. Keep ahead through woodland and down into a combe.

3 A track runs down the bottom of the combe. A detour can be made here for the Blue Ball inn, which is 200 yards down the track and left for 100 yards along a road. Otherwise, bear left and follow the track up the combe for a quarter of a mile.

The Blue Ball is a former coaching inn on the old route from Watchet to Lyme Regis. On coaching routes, inns would hang out a coloured emblem for the (usually illiterate) coach drivers, hence a blue ball hung outside this inn.

Crowcombe Park Gate

Harepath, Crowcombe Park Gate

The 'Drove Road' follows a prehistoric ridgeway along the top of the Quantocks. The tree-lined section is typical of 'enclosure roads', made wide enough for two flocks of sheep to pass. It is also known as the 'Harepath', a Saxon name for a road along which troops were moved, and 'Alfred's Road', a reference to King Alfred's defence of the area in the 9th century.

(4) Just beyond the plantation, fork left up a bridleway. In 300 yards this meets the tree-lined track known as the 'Drove Road' running along the main ridge.

(5) Turn left and follow the track for 500 yards to where you see a bridleway sign to the left. Do not take this but follow the fence back round to the right, where you find another bridleway sign on the opposite side.

(6) Go through the gate and follow the field boundary on your right ahead, straight down to a small gate to Quantock Farm. Before the farmyard, go up through the trees to the right of the farmhouse, then

Triscombe Beeches

dropping down to the drive and following it for about two hundred yards.

7 The route then forks down to the left, dropping down the bottom of the combe past some springs, one of which, half-hidden to the right of the path, is known as St David's Well. Here it meets a substantial track, over heathland and quickly into forest. Follow this track right down the bottom of the combe for a mile.

8 At the bottom (Seven Wells Bridge) there is a house and car park. Turn left to follow the main drive back to your car park in a quarter of a mile.

Quantock Combe (above) and Ramscombe

6 Stogursey

A quick tour of the fascinating village of Stogursey is followed by a long walk over fields to the coast, skirting Hinkley Point nuclear power station and back over marshland.

Level: 🥾 but not short
Length: 12 kms, 7.5 miles
Terrain: Undulating but no steep climbs. Can be wet and muddy.
Park and start: In the High Street near the Acland Hood Arms and Post Office
Start ref: ST203428. Postcode TA5 1TA
Public transport: Reasonable (to Stogursey)
Websites: www.meb39.freeuk.com
www.quantockonline/quantocks/villages

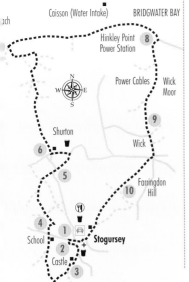

Originally known as plain Stoke, meaning 'church', Stogursey became known as Stoke Coursey through med-ieval ownership of the de Curci family. After the Norman conquest, William de Falaise had given the church to an abbey from Normandy. The monks enlarged it to double as a parish church and priory. In recent times the principal landowners, living at Fairfield, to the west of the village, have been Palmers, Verneys, and Acland-Hoods (after which one of the two pubs is named).

There are two sets of almshouses in the village, the one in Lime Street being built for women and the one in St Andrew's Street for men. Both were restored in the 1980s. On the roof of those in St Andrew's Street is the original "Ding Darling Bell", which was rung daily for the recitation of the Angelus, as requested by their founder in 1414, and is still rung today. The nuclear power station at Hinkley Point now brings employment, although at the time of writing its future is uncertain, with much opposition to a proposed new reactor.

Caisson (Water Intake) BRIDGWATER BAY
Hinkley Point Power Station 8
Power Cables Wick Moor
9
Shurton Wick
6
5 Farringdon Hill
10
4
School 1 Stogursey
2
Castle 3

1 **Set off:** With the Post office on your right and Acland Hood Arms on your left, walk up the street a few yards and bear left by the old cross down St Andrew's Road. Where the road bears left, detour ahead to visit the well.

St Andrew's Well

St Andrew's Well, an ancient holy well, restored in 1979, consists of two springs, formerly used separately for clothes washing and drinking water. In 1870 Sir Peregrine Acland enclosed the area and built the entrance arch.

2 Continue along the road, turning right at the almshouses. Continue along the street for a hundred yards, then bear right towards the castle.

3 At the castle, follow the moat around to the left for another hundred yards to a stile into a field. Keep to the right hand edge of the

Stogursey Castle (left) was rebuilt in the early 12th century by William de Curci. It was damaged a century later and became a farm, with only a few walls and moat remaining. The early 17th century thatched cottage built within the gatehouse is a holiday let belonging to the Landmark Trust.

Stogursey Church (above) and Stogursey School

field, cross another stile and, just before another, turn right through a gate into a field. Go straight ahead over the field, then bear right (N) towards a stile. Cross this and head for the stile and gate to the lane below the school. Take the lane to the road.

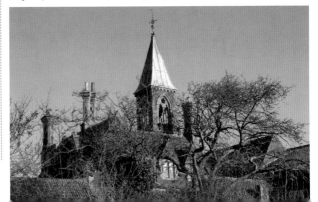

Stogursey School is a stunning example of Victorian Gothic architecture. It was designed by John Norton for Sir Peregrine Acland, who gave the school in 1860 to the community, as a thanks offering for the recovery of his daughter Isabel following a serious illness.

4 Cross the road and go down Town Close opposite. Bear right and, before the next junction, turn left down a footpath between houses. Cross the stile, follow the fence to another, then keep ahead (NW) along the right hand edge of the next few fields, gradually looping around to the right (NE). After a narrow field the route enters a lane.

5 Bear left along the road for a hundred yards, then right along a path. Keep ahead over stiles, then turn left by a stone wall to the street by the Shurton Inn. Turn left along the road for 300 yards, then turn right down a lane beyond some cottages.

Shurton Lane

Hinkley Point

6 Bear right behind the cottages, then left along the edge of a field to rejoin the lane. Keep ahead along the lane for a mile, then go down and to the right of a barn. The route follows the far side of the hedge beyond the barn to the left (SW). From the corner of the hedge, follow it for a quarter of a mile, then bear right (NW) across the field with the edge of an enclosed scrubby area to your left.

Hinkley Beach

The first reactor at Hinkley Point produced electricity from 1965 to 2000. Hinkley Point B will be decommissioned in 2011. There are plans for a Hinkley Point C reactor and a wind farm.

7 At the coast, turn right and follow the Coast Path for two miles, including the concrete walkway around the power station.

8 At the far side of the power station bear right, around the perimeter fence. Follow a rhyne (drainage ditch) ahead and away from the fence. At a junction, bear left over a bridge over the rhyne, then right to

At Shurton Court lived Coleridge's university friend, Henry Poole. The nearby beach was subject of Coleridge's poem 'Lines Written at Shurton Bars.' Since 1954 the coast east of there has formed Bridgwater Bay National Nature Reserve, an important resting and feeding place for migrant birds.

keep the rhyne on your right. Where the rhyne narrows, bear right (SW), following the line of reeds straight under the power cables to a gate leading onto a lane. Follow the lane to the road at Wick.

9 Keep ahead along the road to a junction. Take the cutting straight through to the junction beyond. Turn right along the road, then immediately left up the path across the fields. Keep ahead (SW) up the next field to a stile. Follow the hedge on the right of the next field. Keep ahead (SW) along field boundaries, following footpath signs along the edge of a small woodland.

10 At the far side keep ahead but bear slightly left across the top of the field, diagonally across the next field, then drop to half way down the left side of the next field to a stile and out onto a lane. Turn right, down the lane and ahead to Stogursey parish church. Turn right along the road to return to the High Street.

Reeds Wick Moor

Near Hinkley

7 Nether Stowey

This walk takes in a village, a beautiful church and two castles, apart by over a thousand years in age and a thousand feet in altitude. The stunted oaks around the prehistoric fort provide a strong atmosphere.

Nether Stowey is a centre for the eastern side of the Quantocks. The main streets have cobbled pavements and a stream called by Coleridge 'the dear gutter of Stowey'. The village was a centre of the woollen industry in medieval times and there is a mixture of cottages, shops and houses of different ages.

'Coleridge Cottage' in Lime Street has belonged to the National Trust since 1909. Coleridge and his family lived there in the 1790s, as guests of Thomas Poole, whose house is in Castle Street. Coleridge attracted to 'Stowey' many literary and scientific figures: William and Dorothy Wordsworth, Robert

Level: 🐾 🐾
Length: 9.5 kms, 6 miles
Terrain: A mixture of woodland, open heath and farmland. The first half is all uphill and the second half all downhill but without any very steep sections.
Park and start: Car park next to library and toilets in Castle Street, Nether Stowey
Start ref: ST191397. Postcode TA5 1LN
Public transport: Good (to Nether Stowey)
Websites: www.coleridgeway.co.uk
www.quantockonline.co.uk/quantocks/villages
www.quantockhills.com

Southey, William Hazlitt, Thomas de Quincy and Humphrey Davy. Writer Walter Raymond lived there just after the First World War, recording folk songs and dances and taking friends for walks over the Quantocks.

Map labels: Walford's Gibbet, Nether Stowey, Castle, Broom Squires Cottage, wsborough, Great Bear, Friarn, Over Stowey, A39

Nether Stowey Castle

(1) Set off: Go out of the car park, turning right up Castle Street. Follow the street right up to the top of the hill, where you can detour to visit the castle on the right. Drop down to the next road junction. Turn left along the road. After a hundred yards bear right up the track with the Coleridge Way sign. In half a mile you meet a road by a cottage at Ford.

Nether Stowey Castle, a classic Norman motte and bailey construction, was built in the 11th century and destroyed in the 14th century. A local story is that weird noises can be heard coming from the castle, thought to be the sounds of a sleeping giant.

(2) Turn right, following the Greenway signs up the hill. In about a hundred yards the track levels off. Fork left here, following the Greenway and Coleridge Way signs straight up over the fields and out onto the road at Walford's

Gibbet. Bear left up the road. In a quarter of a mile fork right into the woods, still following the Greenway and Coleridge Way signs. Keep straight ahead (W) and roughly level for nearly a mile, coming out onto a ridge of heathland.

Walford's Gibbet

45

Over Stowey Walled Garden

6 At the church turn left along the road. At the junction 250 yards on, go straight ahead along the track by the walled garden. Keep ahead over the field and along the lane for 200 yards beyond some cottages.

7 Where the lane bears left, turn right into a field. Keep ahead over the field and along a path behind a housing estate. At the road turn left, then right, back down Castle Street to the car park.

The church of St Peter and St Paul at Over Stowey contains fine windows by William Morris and Edward Burne Jones and was visited by Wordsworth and Coleridge. Coleridge had originally intended to settle in the nearby hamlet of Adscombe.

8 **Holford**

A relatively short walk exploring the wooded combes and heath covered ridges around Holford much loved by Coleridge and the Wordsworths and which inspired several poems.

Level: 🥾 🥾
Length: 6 kms, 4 miles
Terrain: Mostly open heath and woodland with two moderate climbs.
Park and start: Parking area in trees by Holford Green. When entering the village from the A39, it is the second turn past the church.
Start ref: ST 154411. Postcode TA5 1RY
Public transport: Good (to Holford)
Websites:
www.quantockonline.co.uk/quantocks/villages
www.quantockhills.com
www.coleridgeway.co.uk

William Wordsworth and his sister Dorothy lived at Alfoxton Park for a year in 1797/98. They were avid walkers and frequently walked to visit Coleridge, ramble up the 'Great Track' over Longstone Hill or take longer walks to Exmoor and beyond. They went out in all weathers and loved the wooded combes around Holford, particularly Hodder's Combe and Holford Combe.

The deep ravine of Holford Glen, once a great tourist attraction, is now a private reserve of the League Against Cruel Sports, but one can peer down into it from this walk. The area has a long tradition of both stag and fox hunting and abounds with red deer. From the 16th to 18th centuries the Glen was a hive of industry, with five water wheels supplying silk mills, by which the area is still known.

49

1 **Set off:** From the car park go back to the road and fork left, keeping the green on your left. In 150 yards you come to an old dog pound.

2 Follow the road round to the right. It then bears left along the edge of woodland and in half a mile it crosses a cattle grid to pass Alfoxton house. Continue up into the woods. 200 yards past the house there is a hairpin bend. Fork left here, up the bottom of the wooded combe. At the heathland at the top, fork right (SW) along the main track for a hundred yards in the direction of Staple Plain.

Alfoxton Coach House

The dog pound near Alfoxton was built after stray dogs caused a commotion one night in the nearby hunt kennels. The huntsman went out in the dark to silence the hounds but they did not recognise him and tore him to pieces.

Deer at Alfoxton House

Beech Trees New Ground

The house at Alfoxton was rebuilt in 1710 by John St Aubyn after a disastrous fire. It has kept much of the style of the period with fine plasterwork and panelling. Since the 1920s it has been a hotel, boys' prep school and Christian holiday home before reverting to a hotel and private house.

Long Stone

3 At a crossing of tracks fork left, taking the narrow path straight up the hill (S). Keep ahead, passing the Long Stone on your right and crossing a track to the track running up the spine of the ridge. Keep straight ahead (S) and gradually downhill, passing to the right of a spur of the hillside and into a steep combe running down into the woods.

4 Turn left on the main track running down the combe. After three hundred yards cross the stream and fork right and round into the next combe. Immediately cross the stream

Stream Sheppard's Combe

in that combe and go ahead up the far valley side. The path zig-zags up and out of the woodland. Go ahead to the top of the near ridge, 250 yards beyond the edge of the wood.

5 A great number of paths join here. You need to keep straight ahead (E) to drop down a small combe with scattered holly

Pollarded tree Lady's Edge

trees. The track follows the bottom of the combe round to the left and joins the main track in the bottom of Holford Combe.

6 Turn left along the lower track. This becomes a road passing Combe House Hotel and running down to a junction at the Triangle. Fork left, around the thatched cottages, to return to the green.

Combe House Hotel

Silk Mill Cottages

Combe House Hotel was formerly a tannery. Its water wheel was built in 1893 and used for pumping fluids to and from the tan pits. The tannery closed soon after but the wheel continued in use until 1953 working machinery and generating electricity.

9 West Quantoxhead

A relatively short circle around the NW end of the Quantock ridge, taking in open heathland with wide views and a variety of woodland.

Level: ♥♥
Length: 8 kms, 5 miles
Terrain: Largely on open heath and plantation, with two long climbs.
Park and start: Staple Plain car park. Staple Plain is signposted from the road junction in West Quantoxhead village. The road becomes a dirt track, passing a plantation on the right and there is a parking area at the end of the plantation.
Start ref: ST117411. Postcode TA4 4EA
Public transport: Good (to West Quantoxhead)
Websites: www.quantockonline.co.uk/quantocks/villages

West Quantoxhead church, former manor house, former village school and the village hall on the coast side of the A39, where most of the village existed until the 19th century. The owners of the manor demolished the village to extend the parkland around the house. The manor belonged to the Mallet family until 1736, when it was sold after a Richard Veale ran off to the West Indies with the tax money they owed the Crown. William Mallet died from a fire at sea, trying to catch up with Veale. The owner of the manor who left the biggest impression was Sir Peregrine Acland, of Fairfield near Stogursey, who purchased the estate in 1836. He altered the Tudor manor house and had the school built, as well as a new church. The house has since been a private girls' school, a Buddhist Centre and now a hotel specialising in weddings.

St Audries / A39 / Deer Park / West Hill / Perry Combe / Smith's Combe / Den's Combe / St Quantoxhead / Staple Plantation / Vinny Combe / Beacon Hill / Longstone Hill / Weacombe Combe / Bicknoller Post

55

Set off: From the car park, facing Staple Plantation, take the path running down from left hand corner of the wall. This drops left into the bottom of Weacombe. Where it meets the main track running down the combe, fork left and follow it up the combe for nearly a mile. The path splits near the top. Keep upwards, bearing to the right to meet a crossing of tracks on the ridge.

2 Go straight over the ridge. Passing the Bicknoller Post on your right and follow a track bearing downhill diagonally to the left (NE). After half a mile another track is joined. Bear sharp left (W). In a few yards, at the top of a small rise, turn sharp right (N) along the path seen running over the top of a ridge.

Riders in Staple Plantation

Follow this for a mile, dropping down a narrower ridge to the fence at the bottom of the open ground.

3 Bear left, following the Greenway and Coleridge Way signs for the next two miles along the edge of open country. The route

Greenway Path

crosses the deep Smith's Combe and drops into the forested Perry Combe.

4 Here follow the Coast Path signs straight ahead (W) in and out of the combe and round through the Deer Park fence into a large plantation. The route follows the bottom of the plantation adjacent to the main road. It comes out in a combe above a cottage. Drop down the combe towards the main road.

5 At the main road the route bears left along a path running parallel with it. At the pub car

The old road from Holford to Williton came up Longstone Hill and there was a building at Bicknoller Post where horses were changed. The current post was erected in 2008, replacing one put in by Harry Coles (from St Audries) in 1929. In keeping with tradition a dated coin was placed under the post.

Smith's Combe

park keep left and uphill on the tarmaced lane. In a hundred yards take the gate ahead, following the path up through the old quarry, keeping the stream to your left for half a mile. Just before the path crosses it, take the path up the steps to the right, bringing you back to the car park.

The present church at St Audries was built in 1854 to replace an unsafe mediaeval building. The rood screen from the former church ended up at Exford whilst a wooden church, erected for the period of construction of the new church, was given to the parish of Stolford, where it remains in use.

Coastline at St Audries

Minehead and Watchet from Staple Plantation

10 **East Quantoxhead**

A relatively easy and very varied walk taking in two villages, coastline, farmland and open heath.

Level: 🐾
Length: 9 kms, 5.5 miles
Terrain: Undulating but not too steep. Some walking on minor roads and much over farmland.
Park and start: Entrance to car park opposite pond at East Quantoxhead.
Start ref: ST137436. Postcode TA5 1EJ
Public transport: Good (to Kilve)
Websites:
www.quantockonline.co.uk/quantocks/villages
www.kilve.ukfossils.co.uk

The East Quantoxhead Estate has been in the hands of the Luttrell family since the early 13th century. They also owned much of Dunster and its castle. Court House dates from the 15th century but much is from the 17th century.

Dorothy Wordsworth wrote of walks in this area: 'Wherever we turn we have woods, smooth downs and valleys with small brooks running down them through meadows scattered over with trees. The hills that cradle these villages are either covered with fern or bilberries or oakwoods – walks extend for miles over the hilltops.' Coleridge and Wordsworth loved Kilve beach. Coleridge called it 'our favourite seat' and Wordsworth wrote about 'Kilve's delightful shore' in his poem 'Anecdote for Fathers.'

Set off: From car park entrance turn right, then left round pond, following signs to beach. Just before metal gate turn left over fields. At cliff top turn right (NE), towards Kilve, following Coast Path signs.

Beach at East Quantoxhead

Follow the cliff top to Kilve beach. Here you can divert left for the beach or continue ahead for the car park with toilets.

Pass through the car park and up the road (SW) past Kilve Chantry and church to Kilve village.

The rocks at Kilve are known as 'Lias', consisting of layers of black, oil rich shale and grey 'Blue Lias' limestone. Of the fossils on the beach, the best known are the coiled shells of ammonites, dating from 200 million years ago.

Pond at East Quantoxhead

Beach at Kilve

The brick building with a chimney at the edge of the car park is an oil retort built in 1924 to extract oil from the shales on the coast. The venture failed two years later due to a lack of capital and high cost of the process.

4 From Sea Lane cross busy main road and go up Putsham Lane opposite. Half a mile up the lane, where it bends right, take the gateway to the left, signed bridleway. After the trees, take the next gate on the left and follow the stream on the right upwards to a gate

through a deer fence. Keep left above the fence. After the walled garden cut across the corner of the field towards a farm track.

5 Take the gate to the right onto a lane. Turn right, cross the cattle grid and follow the lane up

Kilve Chantry

past Alfoxton. It winds up through woods, passes some houses and drops as a path into woods.

(6) At the path junction bear left (NW) along the fence in the direction of Perry. Keep following the Greenway signs for a mile and a half until you drop into a deep combe. Just before two footbridges, bear right (N) through a gate, in the direction of the

Kilve Chantry or Priory was founded in 1329 by Simon de Furneaux for five priests to pray for the souls of his family after death. In the mid 18th century the building was destroyed by a fire intensified by spirits stored there by smugglers.

Above: Smith's Combe

Below: Path to Higher Street

A39. Keep to the right of a barn, then cross the stream and follow it to the cottages at Higher Street.

(7) Cross the busy main road at the cross roads and follow the minor road towards East Quantoxhead for a quarter of a mile. Where the road bends left take the stile left to cross the field diagonally (NE) to a

gate. Cross the road and take the gate opposite. Cross the fields in the direction of the church. Just before the church take the track, right, to skirt the yard to the car park.

East Quantoxhead Church